T0209788

The
Christmas
Clock

AMY JOYCE

Illustrated by: Violet Slocombe

Copyright © 2022 Amy Joyce.

All rights reserved. No part of this book may be used or reproduced by any means, graphic, electronic, or mechanical, including photocopying, recording, taping or by any information storage retrieval system without the written permission of the author except in the case of brief quotations embodied in critical articles and reviews.

WestBow Press books may be ordered through booksellers or by contacting:

WestBow Press
A Division of Thomas Nelson & Zondervan
1663 Liberty Drive
Bloomington, IN 47403
www.westbowpress.com
844-714-3454

Because of the dynamic nature of the Internet, any web addresses or links contained in this book may have changed since publication and may no longer be valid. The views expressed in this work are solely those of the author and do not necessarily reflect the views of the publisher, and the publisher hereby disclaims any responsibility for them.

Any people depicted in stock imagery provided by Getty Images are models, and such images are being used for illustrative purposes only.
Certain stock imagery © Getty Images.

ISBN: 978-1-6642-6124-2 (sc)
ISBN: 978-1-6642-6125-9 (e)

Library of Congress Control Number: 2022905106

Print information available on the last page.

WestBow Press rev. date: 5/12/2022

WestBow
PRESS®
A DIVISION OF THOMAS NELSON
& ZONDERVAN

This book is dedicated to my friend, Alison Lorkowski who encouraged and believed in me. Her life was full of excitement, joy and honor for God and His Kingdom. Her reward is great and her absence is felt by many this side of glory!

There once was an old **wooden clock**, he sat on the mantle chiming tick tock.

The family within, loved to listen to him and watch the hours grow dim.

One day he noticed a crack, it ran down the middle of his back. He said with dismay, they'll throw me away, because now I'm starting to sway.

After hearing an old man pray, it completely blew him away. He thought it too good to be true, a God who could make you brand new! He knew in his heart it could mean a new start, so he asked God to help him and prayed.

It wasn't long before his flaw was seen, he could tell he was starting to lean. He began to worry but knew God would hurry, so he held onto faith and what that would mean.

Christmas season had just begun, people were preparing for all of the fun. The creche and the garland came out. On the mantle they were scattered about.

A small voice from the back of the room asked why there wasn't a cross and a tomb? She was told it's about Jesus birth, the hope that He gives us on earth. At least we should put up a cross, said the little girl they nicknamed "the Boss".

That gave the old man a thought, he could fix
that old clock that he bought. He took it away
and worked on it later that day. He whittled
and glued and after many small screws placed
it back on the mantle to tell the good news.

A calm peace covered the room, it was the perfect display. The old man filled the crack with what held Jesus back as he hung on the cross that day. The thin cross kept the clock together, stood high like the storms we can weather. The babe born had an extreme cost to pay, He would sacrifice His life and show us the way.

The family sang to the King in the manger, the one who is never a stranger. The clock chimed in glee and overshadowed the tree as he held the symbol Christ paid for you and me!

Is there anything happening in your life that you need to ask God for help with?

Can you think of anyone who needs your prayers today?

Have you done anything for someone else or God today?

What is something you are thankful for.

Tell me about a time when God answered one of your prayers.

When you are worried, what can you remember about God that helps you trust him?

Can you remember a time God blessed you?

What can you do to have a good and godly day?

Remember, faith in God is believing He can and will do all that He has promised. Faithfulness is holding on to that belief even in the face of something scary. A person who has faith in God chooses to love and obey Him no matter what. Prayer is the way you talk to God and how you get to know him and his love for you.

Printed in the United States
by Baker & Taylor Publisher Services